Facets

Margret,
Good Bless
I thank you

Facets

Robin L. Mills

Contents

Introduction

ভ

Feel my passion
See my pain
Bask in my sunshine
Run from my rain
Explore my wisdom
My ignorance ignore
For these are some of my facets
But I hold many more!

ভ

True Friend

ભ્

Although we don't see each other everyday
I just had to take a moment to say
You're in my heart
You're in my mind
I know good friends are hard to find
But in you
I know I've found
The kind of friend that's always around
So in my times
Be it good or bad
In my moments
Rather happy or sad
To have a friend like you makes me glad!

ભ્

Different

ભ

Hey, you don't
Look like me
So why do I imagine
You to be
Similar to the way
I am
I get mad
Because you don't
Think the same
Dress the same
Or see all things
As I do
But then I say
I love you
And say
That it is true
Then I get mad
When you ask me
Why can't I love you for you!

ભ

Oh Boy

❧

I romance the idea of love with no end
I think of you being more than a friend
I wish you looked at me in the same
But because you don't
Who is to blame?
I know I can't go on with this guessing game
I thought for sure you would be true
I've found you're not and I don't know what to do
I want so much to communicate
I'd really like to do this before it's too late
I ask you questions to no avail
I get answers that make me think I've got a tail
You handle the situation like it's all about you
To tell the truth my dear, that is not true
I would give you your worth with no trouble at all
I would come immediately when you call
I can see none of this has any strength
So I guess what I'm saying is we've run our length!

❧

Patience

For so many things
I pray to Thee
I ask you to make me a better me
So many times I want you to hurry
When I think it's time
And you don't, I worry
I know all good will come in time
But your time
And mine don't always rhyme
I want everything for a specific time or date
But through you I've learned to sit back and wait
When my prayer is answered I should appreciate
This lesson was not easy at all
For many times I did stumble and fall
You'd pick me up because you heard my call
With this lesson under my belt
I want to say "Thank you"
And your presence is always felt!

Awakened

To visualize
Is to realize
You have the ability
To fantasize
Visualization
Is the stimulation
Of your own realization
To visualize isn't to find the source
It's only acknowledging
The chosen course
The realization is the force
That makes me find the resource
As my mind drifts through
The fertilization
That causes my life much constipation
I notice a scheme
Or so it may seem
I spend too much time
On a dream!

Darkness

ॐ

I embrace the darkness of the night
With so much joy
Not an iota of fright
I feel the peacefulness
Flowing through the air
This is the time I have not a worry or care
I sit and think
And know in my heart
That tomorrow brings my life
To a brand new start!

ॐ

Explore

છ

Open your heart
Open your mind
You'll be surprised
By the treasures you'll find
We keep so much locked away
It's not always good
To save for a rainy day
We have so much in
That should be let out
You'll feel much better
And that's no doubt
The more you keep
The worse you feel
It causes confusion
That's very real
So reach inside
Speak from your heart and mind
Only then will true peace be
A precious find!

છ

Oops

CR

We share the idea of the perfect world
The perfect boy
The perfect girl
We all know how to do things in the perfect way
The perfect style
The right thing to say
We all share the same obsession
That is the great desire for perfection
But as it is and truth be told
That idea is ages old
At some point in life we settle on the best we can
And if that's not good enough
We'll sometimes pretend
As we pretend we settle for less
We never get perfection
And fall short on the best!

CR

Kindness

They say be kind to others you meet
One day you may be the one with no feet.
They say respect those that are older
For you never know when your body may get colder
They say teach lessons to all those that listen
By doing so, someone's life may glisten
They say feed the hungry
Clothe the poor
By doing these things in your life
You're opening a new door
You're encouraging another to feel good
You're helping someone that may be misunderstood
It's okay to help another get back on their way
In doing so, good luck is never far away!

Peace

Let me govern
The weather in my life
By controlling the rain
The thing called strife
Let me control the way it shall fall
Matter of fact I think not at all
Let me seek and find the sun
Remove the troubles
Connect with One
In my life I want to be free
Governed only by the one that be!

Mixed

❧

You say you
Know me
I think you should
But damn, I'm so
Misunderstood
I think you see
Who you wish you were
And you try to mold
Me into her
The saddest part
But the truth too
Please tell me
Who the hell are you?

❧

Regroup

രു

Power to the people
Power from one,
Let's keep running the race,
Until we've won,
Don't sell out to clothes, gadgets and such,
In the truth there is power,
We're losing touch,
You think the truth is all outside,
You're in the wrong place,
Let's stop trying to hide,
For what's real is all within,
You're missing the point people,
Shall we start again?
Disrobe, let go of all that's not real,
Don't be afraid to show, reveal,
Share what you hold,
The real you,
If you don't use it,
You'll never make it through!

രു

Listen

Do I speak words of nature?
I say do I speak words of nature?
Ah, but you laugh at me,
Do I speak words of nature?
Sounds funny to thee,
Because you listen to each and every word
The words of nature go unheard
You missed the one this morning
Telling you your day would be fine
Words of nature are spoken softly
Never loud or in a boisterous way,
Words of nature are sometimes silent,
Only there for us to feel,
If you pay close attention,
You too will know they are words that are real!

Easy

❧

Move in silence
As every fight doesn't deserve a punch
Move in peace
Every tide doesn't need another wave
Move calmly
Every storm doesn't need more wind
Move with grace
Every argument doesn't need more words
Move in peace
As every corner of the world needs some
Move in love
Until all the wars are won!
Be the ray of sun,
The star of hope,
The gentleness to help all cope!

❧

Change

ભ્ર

All that was,
Is no more,
Move on my friend,
Close that door,
Venture on in life,
There is much more,
Allowing things to stay the same,
Won't make you better,
Won't change the game,
Many times we're afraid to grow,
In order to prosper,
You must move along,
The future is yours to use and be strong!

ભ્ર

Misfit

☞

I think of you in all aspects
Trying to leave out disrespect
I think of you in surrounding area
Damn you just don't meet the criteria
I think of you hanging with me
Seems when it happens intellect must flee
I think of you as the type to wed
Thought goes away
But you're in my bed
My bed oh yeah that's it
Cause in my life
It's the only place you fit!

☞

Wanted

Get help is what they say
Let me tell you what happened today
I say fact
They say fiction
OK wait a minute I'll give you a description
My eye was puffy and black
They say ma'am we need more fact
So my arm was black and blue
They say
We want to believe what you say is true
After an hour talking to the crew
They say 'til next time there's nothing we can do
I rushed home in despair
All day long I found no one to care
Again I spent another night
My whole body shaken with fright
Now I speak to you from above
After another brutal beating
All I wanted was love!

History

CR

L-A-D-Y a word from the past
No longer used, cause we're skipping class
Gotta ride on those 24's
Don't need no one opening doors
We sacrifice all that is good
To be one of the girls from the hood
We give up what's precious and true
But for real that's nothing new
No longer do we use discretion
Got no time for affection
Slinging and blinging is what it's all about
Going home ain't it
I gotta be out
Ain't thinking bout being no scholar
Check me out, I'm a baller, holler!
L-A-D-Y ain't nothin' I know
Gotta move fast, can't go slow
Movin' so fast I didn't realize
I'm seventeen got bags under my eyes
Now I'm big with my second kid
Not even sure what I did
Sometimes now I wanna cry
Cause Grandma always said, be an L-A-D-Y!

CR

Wish

ⓒⓡ

Say a death wish
Ain't what you had
Said you're just another good one
Gone bad
Looking at the picture
Wish that was true
Why'd you do
The stuff you do
Said you were pretty
Fine and such
Always had to go further
Than a little touch
Couldn't just be
Visually elected
Had to go all the way
Unprotected
Did it over and over again
Always calling the culprit a friend
Let 'em dive in
Swim like a fish
But you keep saying
You don't have a death wish!

ⓒⓡ

Touch

ೞ

Touch me,
Yes touch me there
You say you can't
Or you don't dare,
Along the way
We've had ups and downs
Many feelings met with smiles and frowns
You think you love me,
Oh don't you dare
You've got it twisted
You merely care,
I fill a void,
A little hole,
At night I keep you from being cold,
One day as I was driving along,
Suddenly it hit me,
I became aware,
I realized you only care,
Because if it was love
You could touch me there!

ೞ

Hidden

Today take yourself
On a silent journey
To an area deep within
Yes I need you to go past your heart
To that special area
That special part
The area that is kept well concealed
The area of you
That is so real
The area that scares you the most
In there, there is no need to boast
Relax your mind,
Just let it coast
It's the area
That holds your strength
It's where all your purities reside
It's the area that holds the beauty
That really caught my eye!

Déjà Vu

As our eyes meet on a subway train
My heart fills with passion and pain
The passion is for the person I knew
The one I loved, oh so true
The pain is for all I feel
My heart breaking 'cause you ain't real
The passion and pain both are not new
But I still hold them deep inside just for you!

Puzzle

CR

I've seen many moons
Sat in crowded rooms
Shared an empty heart
Cried a lot of tears
Now as I reminisce
I try to see where it all makes sense
I see how it all joins as one
Although some did bring me fun
Many brought me strife
It's all been events
At one time or another
In my wonderful life!

CR

Distance

So many times with paper and pen
I've express myself again and again
There is difference between now and then
I knew you as lover, but you were really a friend
Although the second should be the first
I always thought our relationship was cursed
It never got better only worse
Seems our anger was repeated, rehearsed
Then I left you and went away
No need to fight, no need to stay
I had to put distance in my part of the play
I worship you better from afar
I can do it now without a scar
And although the lover thing can never happen again
With time and distance I can at least call you a friend.

Lesson

☌

I've learned to forgive
Now, I can give.
I've learned to love
Now, I can live!

☌

Funny

Hell fire
Damn a bear
I can't find my underwear
Went to the woods
Got a scare
I believe
I left them there!

Today

ОЗ

Today I listen
Today I pray
Today I have so much to say
But like any other day
Today must go away
And when tomorrow is new
I'll feel I have much to do
And as I go along my way
Once again it will be today!

ОЗ

Do I

Free is something we all strive to be
No one wants to deal with the price you see
To be free may require loneliness
Many hours of onlyness
Free requires no one to share
And many hours to spare
No one to call your own
Many nights of empty home
To me free has a very high price
Although compromise calls for sacrifice
It's an essential to me
I will compromise and share you see
Because truthfully I just don't want to be free!

Again

&

If I had a moment
To do it all again
Could I do it all over
Could I really win
Again may never come
Yes, chances are slim
But in my heart I know
The feeling from within
If given the opportunity
And time would be our friend
I would certainly without hesitation
Kiss you over and over, Again!

&

Pain

I felt a tear
Roll down my cheek
Just before it started to rain
My heart was so heavy
My mind was full pain
Once I thought you were a gain
My heart and soul
My everything
Today I see you
With my own eyes
In the arms of another
And it makes me cry!

Lost

ଜେ

My nights are dark
My days are cold
I am young
In a world of old
I try to understand
An unwritten plan
A guideline of rules
That aren't taught anywhere
Not even in schools
I'm given no idea
Not even a clue
I'm out in the world
And don't know what to do!

ଜେ

One Side

I've heard many stories of pain
And how others
Have done you wrong
Sometimes the convo reminds me
Of a rather old song
There's stories of mistreatment
Filled with lies and deceit
They are filled
With seemingly negative people
I'd never want to meet
But as I listen closely
Yes, really lend an ear
Only one side of the story
Is what I get to hear!

Wish

○੨

Tonight as I close my eyes to sleep
I'll ask for another day
I'll ask for peace
And understanding
And for stress to go away
I'll ask for many little things
That I want to be shared by many
I'll ask for the turmoil to be gone
And know tomorrow will not hold any!
A creative mind
Is much like
A closed book
It can go unnoticed
If no one
Takes a look
Allowing the mind to open
And be very free
Allowing it to express
Its treasures
For the world to see
I just had to say
"Thank you,"
Commend you for being wise
Now the book is open
Full of wisdom and surprise!

○੨

Growing

Looking at me
Is like looking at a tree
Room for growth
Much more to see
Understanding at times
We must lose a branch
To give newness and change
A chance
Realizing only when I reach deep within
Can my growth process
Happen again and again!

Here

CR

To look at self
Is reality
Something we're not
Always ready to see
It causes fear
Sometimes shame
Reminding us
How deep we're in the game
The game of life
The game of sometimes no win
But we're forced to play
Again and again
The hand we're dealt
Often times with no aces
Where people leave us
With no traces
We look at self
Sometimes shedding a tear
But hell move over world
I'm strong, I'm here!

CR

Lesson

I learned of sex too early
And love rather late
For so many years
I mistook one for the other
What a mistake
I wonder in the world today
How many others
Are being taught this way
As I sit and converse
And the truth be told
When I was learning this
It was already old!

Misguided

I am little
Why are you leaving me here
I am but a child
I am full of fear
You tell me
It will all be okay
Then suddenly you turn
And walk away
I thought you were
My provider and protector
Actually you were my first molester!

Tree

It's winter time
And I'm all alone
They no longer call me home
I've no ability to offer shade
Even color has started to fade
My covers have fallen
And been blown away
I guess I'm feeling lonely today
I stand here before you
Very strong
And know in my roots
It won't be long
Again I will be
Another season of beautiful me
If you haven't guessed
I'm a tree!

Chance

My mind, my heart
Most certainly a major part
My soul is the ultimate force
As it holds the guiding light
The insight, the course
I neglect it, let its signs subside
Then wonder why I'm caught
On a wild ride
I never take a moment
To listen within
But today I ask
For one more chance again!

Forever

Friends now
Friends to the end
For so many years
That's how it's been
You're always there
And this I know
But I had to take a moment
To say, "I love you so"
You know my secrets
Past and present
All there is to me
I always want you to know
I'm very thankful we came to be!

Star

ᐸᔆ

While enjoying the silence
Of a cloud filled night
My eyes gazed upon a lone star
As I envisioned its beauty
My mind drifted afar
Wondering how many others
Shared the beauty of that star
Wondering if anyone saw its glow
Was it the same star
My ancestors came to know
My mind drifted many places
Near and far
While enjoying the light
Of a lone star!

ᐸᔆ

End

As summer beauty
Gives way to a marvelous fall
I sit back and reminisce
Over it all
Beautiful sunsets
Over an ocean blue
Whispers of a breeze
Just passing through
Colorful flowers
Drifting in the wind
Hoping they will
Come back again
The feeling of sand
Beneath my feet
Enjoying evening waters
After a day of heat
As I watch the summer
Come to a close
I'll cling to the memory
Like summer's final rose!

Reality

CR

I cover my heart
Put my thoughts aside
But I know this is going to be a long ride
Not sure if it will always be a scenic route
As I am learning what you're all about
Suddenly I take a moment and regress
Am I denying myself happiness
Should I just go forward in glee
Hoping you will never hurt me
Or maybe I can play it by ear
And just be thankful that you're here
So much thought is put on our mind
Knowing the heart wins every time!

CR

Blessing

Welcome to my world
Glad to see you again
You ask me how I've been
I wonder where to start
Aside from being broke
And occasionally falling apart
I'm able to greet each day
With a peace filled
Welcoming heart
I've learned over time
Life may not always rhyme
There's moments when I'd rather hide
But it's life so I enjoy the ride
I've experienced a bump or two
But I reach inside and see it through
And as I continue to embrace each lesson
I've come to realize life is the grandest blessing!

Rain

Fragrances of a fresh rain
Play so gently on my brain
It dampens my body
And moistens my soul
Clearing all thoughts
That burdened my existence
Causing me to meet life
With a strong resistance
The rain does so much for me
It always clears my path
And lets me be free!

Move

We speak of many things
That stand in our way
But what are they really
Might I say
Do we find doubt in self
Hindering us from reaching
Higher wealth
Do we have low self esteem
Feeling we are not worthy
Of living our dream
Often times we feel less
Allowing our lives to become a mess
Realize the only thing standing
In your way
Is the one you see in the mirror
Every day!

Family

The family consists
Of a husband and wife
Sometime ago
That was the perfect life
Today this is strange
Rarely true
In many cases
One parent will have to do
Often times
It's parents no more
Your grands meet you
When you come through the door
The family structure has drastically changed
Today the whole situation has been rearranged!

Decision

What is there to do with a dream
Do you chase it
Share it with another
Make your bed in the morning
And leave it under the cover
Really you see
The dream is yours
It's up to you
To let it open or close doors!

Beauty

ෆ

Bam, it's reality
All in your face
So much has changed
It's a brand new place
Big Mama's has been replaced
With Chin's
Down the street it's Mexican
Latino, Asian, European, African
We've come together to keep it
American
Together we make the rainbow glow
Together we're so beautiful, you know!

ෆ

Deceit

෬

I came from love
I came from trust
Really I came from lust

I came from truth
I came from care
Really I came from a woman in despair

I came from honor
I came from wealth
Really it's a blessing I have good health

I came in a world with many deceptions
Didn't even have a warm reception
Now I live my life trying to make many corrections!

෬

All I have,
Is all I need
As I need more,
So shall I receive!

Robin Lynn Mills
12/07/2007

Made in the USA